pilgrim

THE COMMANDMENTS
A COURSE FOR THE CHRISTIAN JOURNEY

Church Publishing
NEW YORK

Authors and Contributors

Authors

Stephen Cottrell is the Bishop of Chelmsford
Steven Croft is the Bishop of Sheffield
Paula Gooder is a leading New Testament writer and lecturer
Robert Atwell is the Bishop of Stockport
Sharon Ely Pearson is a Christian educator in The Episcopal Church

Contributors

Joanne Grenfell is Archdeacon of Portsdown in the Diocese of Portsmouth
J. John is a renowned international Christian speaker and author
Victoria Matthews is the Bishop of Christ Church, New Zealand
Alan Smith is the Bishop of St Albans
Andrew Watson is the Bishop of Aston in the Diocese of Birmingham
Lucy Winkett is the Rector of St James Piccadilly, Diocese of London

pilgrim

THE COMMANDMENTS
A COURSE FOR THE CHRISTIAN JOURNEY

STEPHEN COTTRELL
STEVEN CROFT
PAULA GOODER
ROBERT ATWELL
SHARON ELY PEARSON

Contributions from
JOANNE GRENFELL   J. JOHN
VICTORIA MATTHEWS   ALAN SMITH
ANDREW WATSON   LUCY WINKETT

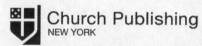

Church Publishing
NEW YORK

First published in the United Kingdom in 2014 by

Church House Publishing
Church House
Great Smith Street
London SW1P 3AZ

First published in the United States in 2016 by

Church Publishing, Incorporated.
19 East 34th Street
New York, New York 10016
www.churchpublishing.org

Cover and contents design by David McNeill, Revo Design.

Library of Congress Cataloging-in-Publication Data:

A record of this book is available from the Library of Congress.

ISBN-13: 978-0-89869-942-5 (pbk.)
ISBN-13: 978-0-89869-943-2 (ebook)

Printed in the United States of America

CONTENTS

WELCOME TO *PILGRIM*

Welcome to this course of exploration into the truth of the Christian faith as it has been revealed in Jesus Christ and lived out in his Church down through the centuries.

The aim of this course is to help people explore what it means to become disciples of Jesus Christ. From the very beginning of his ministry, Jesus called people to follow him and become his disciples. The Church in every generation shares in the task of helping others hear Christ's call to them and follow him.

We hope the course will help you to understand this faith and to see how it can be lived out each day, and that it will equip you to make a decision about whether to be part of this Church. This will either happen by being baptized and confirmed, if this has not happened to you before, or by a renewal of baptismal vows.

You won't be able to find out everything about the Christian faith in any one course. But through the *Pilgrim* course material you will be able to reflect on some of the great texts that have been particularly significant to Christian people from the earliest days of the Church:

- The Creeds
- The Lord's Prayer
- The Beatitudes
- The Commandments

There is one book based on each of these texts in the "Follow" stage of *Pilgrim* (designed for absolute beginners) and one that goes further in the "Grow" (discipleship) stage.

By learning these texts, reflecting upon them, and seeing what they mean for your life, you will make a journey through the great story of the Christian faith. And you will do this in the company of a small group of fellow travelers: people like you who want to find out more about the Christian faith and are considering its claims and challenges.

In other words, this course is for people who are *not yet Christians*, but who are open to finding out more and *for those who are just beginning the journey*. People who want some sort of *refresher course* are also very welcome. In walking with you on this journey we are not assuming that you necessarily share the beliefs that are being explored, just that you want to find out about them.

This course will approach the great issues of faith not by trying to persuade you to believe, but by encouraging you to practice the ancient disciplines of biblical reflection and prayer that have always been at the heart of the living out of Christian faith.

We don't think these are things that should only be practiced once you have come to faith. Rather, they can be the means by which faith is received and then strengthened within us.

Each book has six or seven sessions, and in each session you will find:

- a **theme**
- some **opening prayers**
- a **"conversation-starter"**
- an opportunity to **reflect** on a **reading** from Scripture (the Bible)
- a short **article** from a contemporary Christian writer on the theme
- some **questions** to address
- a further time of **prayer**
- finally, a **"sending out"** section, with suggestions for further reflection and selected quotations from the great tradition of Christian writing to help you do so.

This pattern of contemplation and discussion will, we believe, help you to decide whether you wish to respond to Christ and be part of his Church. Remember that the Church is not a group of men and women who are, themselves, certain about all these things, but who "believe, with God's help" (this is what you are asked at baptism) and then go on following Jesus Christ and continuing the journey of faith.

We all learn in different ways and there is a variety of material here to support you. Different people will receive something from the different parts of the session according to their own learning style.

At the end of this course, we hope you will have made some new friends and explored quite a lot of areas of Christian faith. Just as importantly, you will have been given confidence to read the Bible prayerfully and critically, and you will have, if you wish, established a pattern for prayer. We hope that *Pilgrim* will help you lay a foundation for a lifetime of learning more about God's love revealed in Jesus Christ and what it means to be his disciple.

This little book gives you all you need to begin this great journey. You are standing where millions of men and women have stood: you have caught a glimpse of who God is, and you are puzzled and curious to know whether the claims of the Christian faith can be trusted and whether they actually make any difference to life.

This book and this course can help you. You will need the book for each session, but outside of the sessions you may want to look each week at the material you are about to study together. As the course goes on, you may want to take time each week to look back at what you have already covered as you move forward on your own pilgrimage.

INTRODUCTION TO *THE COMMANDMENTS*

Following Jesus is about the way we act as well as what we believe. So how should Christians act and how should we live?

This part of *Pilgrim* explores that question through one of the core texts of the Christian faith: the Commandments. We look in Session 1 at the two commandments Jesus uses to summarize the whole of the Old Testament law: the call to love God and to love our neighbor as ourselves. In Sessions 2-6 we explore the remainder of the Ten Commandments.

The Ten Commandments and Jesus' summary of the law were at one time near the very center of our culture and civilization. They were learned by heart and often rehearsed in public worship. They were inscribed in public places and often displayed in the home. For centuries they were at the center of what Christians learned about their faith. Yet today they are little known and understood, let alone followed.

Another name for the Ten Commandments is the Decalogue or "Ten Words." The text of the Commandments is found in two places in the Bible. In Exodus 20:1-17, God speaks these words after the people of Israel have consecrated themselves at Mount Sinai. They are inscribed on two tablets of the covenant, "written with the finger of God," the first and most important part of the Law of God, and they are a gift of God to the people of Israel—and through them to the whole of humankind.

The same Ten Commandments are repeated in Deuteronomy 5:6-21 (with some variations). In Deuteronomy, Moses looks back and interprets the law for the people of God in every generation. Again, these Ten Commandments are in first place and given supreme importance in the whole of Scripture.

The Ten Commandments are a very short text and a memorable one. They are laws entrusted to a community of people who have been rescued from slavery, a people who have been saved from their enemies through the crossing of the Red Sea, a people called into a special covenant relationship with God, and who are now learning to live in freedom as they journey to the Promised Land.

In the same way, from the early days of the Church, they have been taught to those preparing for baptism as one of the foundations of our faith. Like the Israelites, we have been rescued from slavery to sin and death through the death of Jesus on the cross and his resurrection. We have passed through the waters of baptism. We are called into a new covenant and a special relationship with God as part of the Church. We are learning to live in holiness and freedom as we journey through this life to the home God has prepared for us.

It is still helpful to think of the Ten Commandments as written on two tablets. By and large, the first tablet deals with our relationship and obligations to God and the second deals with our obligations and relationships to other people. There have been different ways of "numbering" the commandments in different churches down the centuries, but we follow here the numbering as normally followed in Episcopal churches.

Jesus' great summary of the law is found in Mark 12:28-34, Matthew 22:34-40, and Luke 10:25-38. The first of the two commandments Jesus quotes is from Deuteronomy 6:5. It is from a passage called the "Shema," still recited to this day by orthodox Jews (the title is taken from the Hebrew word "Hear," which is the first word of the text). This first commandment sums up in a positive form the first tablet of the Decalogue.

Jesus' second commandment, quoted from Leviticus 19:18, is taken from another great summary of the law sometimes known as The Holiness Code because of its frequent reference to the holiness of God. This second great commandment sums up in a positive form the second tablet of the Decalogue about the ways in which we should act towards other people.

It's vital for our Christian lives that these two tablets and the two greatest commandments are held together. As Christian disciples, we cannot focus on love for God and neglect the way we act towards our neighbors. Nor should we focus on the way we act towards our neighbors and neglect our love for God. The two need to be held together. Our lives need to be shaped in a rhythm of worship and service: love for God and love for others.

Unlike Jesus' summary of the law, eight of the commandments are all framed in the negative: "You shall have no other gods but me... You shall not steal." The Church has always interpreted the negative in the Ten Commandments as having a positive emphasis and the positive as having a negative: both are implied. One of the old catechisms used in the Protestant Churches asks three questions of each commandment:

● What is the commandment?
● What are the duties required in the commandment?
● What are the sins forbidden in the commandment?

The Commandments, like all Scripture, need to be interpreted in order to be understood and used by the Church and by individual Christians. Our understanding of the Commandments is informed by other parts of the Scriptures. They especially need to be interpreted through the life and ministry and teaching of Jesus, who says to his disciples:

"Do not think that I have come to abolish the law or the prophets; I have come not to abolish but to fulfill" (Matthew 5:17).

We will explore in these studies the ways in which Jesus interprets the various commandments for his disciples and expands their meaning (see, for example, Matthew 5:21-30 for an interpretation of the commandments about murder and adultery). However, Christians also read the Ten Commandments today through the lens of the life of Jesus described in the Gospels and the lens of the other New Testament writings. The Ten Commandments, in the form of the Decalogue, are often included in Sunday worship during Lent, the season of penitence (repentance for what wrongs we may have done) before Easter, helping us remember the commandments God gave to us. The people respond, "Amen. Lord have mercy" (see pp. 13-14).

In all of our reflections on how Christians are to live it is important to be clear that we are not made right with God through keeping laws and rules. We cannot earn God's favor or God's love in that way. As Christians, our lives can only be set right with God through God's grace and forgiveness extended to us through the death of Jesus on the cross. Our part in receiving that forgiveness, as we have seen, is repentance and faith and receiving God's gift of the Spirit.

Yet the Ten Commandments do have a part to play. They are given to remind us before and after we become Christians of how our lives fall short of God's standards and how much we need God's forgiveness in Christ. They are given to teach us how we should then aim to live as individuals and as a community.

The standards for life they hold out to us teach us that the Christian life is about far more than keeping external rules. The Commandments demonstrate that growing in Christian grace is about the forming of Christian character and virtue over the whole of our lives. We are not called only to obey laws, but to be Christ-like.

We simply cannot do this on our own. To live by these Commandments we need, in Jeremiah's words, a new heart and a new Spirit, to be transformed from within (Jeremiah 31:33). We need the Holy Spirit to grow within us the fruits of love, joy, peace, patience, kindness, goodness, faithfulness, gentleness, and self-control (Galatians 5:22-23). We need the love and support of a Christian community, however imperfect, to show us the meaning of the Commandments as they are lived out in the reality of life today.

May God bless you and those you journey with in this part of *Pilgrim*.

A NOTE ON THE OPENING WORSHIP

The opening worship for each session uses verses from Psalm 119, the longest of the Psalms. Psalm 119 is an acrostic (or alphabet-based) poem, divided into twenty-two sections of eight verses each. Every line in each section of the psalm begins with the same letter of the alphabet in Hebrew in order (A for verses 1-8, B for verses 9-16, etc.). The whole psalm is a celebration of the law of God and every line of every section contains some reference to that law.

THE COMMANDMENTS

Hear these commandments which God has given to his people, and examine your hearts.

I am the Lord your God who brought you out of bondage.
You shall have no other gods but me.
Amen. Lord have mercy.

You shall not make for yourself any idol.
Amen. Lord have mercy.

You shall not invoke with malice the Name of the Lord your God.
Amen. Lord have mercy.

Remember the Sabbath day and keep it holy.
Amen. Lord have mercy.

Honor your father and your mother.
Amen. Lord have mercy.

You shall not commit murder.
Amen. Lord have mercy.

You shall not commit adultery.
Amen. Lord have mercy.

You shall not steal.
Amen. Lord have mercy.

You shall not be a false witness.
Amen. Lord have mercy.

You shall not covet anything that belongs to your neighbor.
Amen. Lord have mercy.

THE DECALOGUE II: THE BOOK OF COMMON PRAYER, 1979 (P. 350)

SESSION ONE:
PRIORITIES

pilgrim

In this session we explore Jesus' summary of the law as the foundation for the way a disciple is called to live.

Opening Prayers

Your word is a lantern to my feet
And a light upon my path.

PSALM 119:105

You laid down your commandments,
that we should fully keep them.

O, that my ways were made so direct
that I might keep your statutes!

Then should I not be put to shame,
because I regard all your commandments.

I will thank you with an unfeigned heart,
when I have learned your righteous judgments.

I will keep your statutes;
do not utterly forsake me.

PSALM 119:4-8

Almighty God,
We thank you for the gift of your holy word.
May it be a lantern to our feet,
a light to our path
and a strength to our lives.
Take us and use us
to love and serve all people
in the power of the Holy Spirit
and in the name of your Son,
Jesus Christ our Lord. **Amen.**

Conversation

Without looking, how many of the Ten Commandments can you name as a group? Which are the most important and why?

Reflecting on Scripture

Reading

One of the scribes came near and heard them disputing with one another, and seeing that he answered them well, he asked him, "Which commandment is the first of all?" [29]Jesus answered, "The first is, 'Hear, O Israel: the Lord our God, the Lord is one; [30]you shall love the Lord your God with all your heart, and with all your soul, and with all your mind, and with all your strength.' [31]The second is this, 'You shall love your neighbor as yourself.' There is no other commandment greater than these." [32]Then the scribe said to him, "You are right, Teacher; you have truly said that 'he is one, and besides him there is no other'; [33]and 'to love him with all the heart, and with all the understanding, and with all the strength,' and 'to love one's neighbor as oneself,'—this is much more important than all whole burnt offerings and sacrifices." [34]When Jesus saw that he answered wisely, he said to him, "You are not far from the kingdom of God." After that no one dared to ask him any question.

MARK 12:28-34

Explanatory note

At the time of Jesus, a scribe was someone who, in a largely illiterate culture, was able to read and write. As a result, scribes are thought to have been the people who read and interpreted the law for others. It is possible that the priests from the temple were scribes when they were not on duty in the temple.

The word "teacher" is important here as the scribe is acknowledging Jesus' authority as a teacher. The original word used was probably "Rabbi."

Whole burnt-offerings (otherwise called Holocausts) and sacrifices were how God was worshipped in the temple. Here the scribe is acknowledging that what you do is even more important than how you worship God.

● Read the passage through once.

● Keep a few moments' silence.

- Read the passage a second time with different voices.
- Invite everyone to say aloud a word or phrase that strikes them.
- Read the passage a third time.
- Share together what this word or phrase might mean and what questions it raises.

Reflection ANDREW WATSON

Living well

"He never did anyone any harm." It was the most generous tribute that an elderly woman could pay to her husband after 55 years of marriage. The context was a funeral visit, so my next question remained unspoken. But there it was, lingering at the back of my mind: "Yes, but did he ever do anyone any good?"

The widow's tribute reflects an approach to living shared by many: that provided we don't hurt anyone, we've lived well. As an approach it has its roots in the various *"you shall nots"* of the Bible that we'll be looking at later in this book—"You shall not kill," "You shall not commit adultery," and so on. As an approach too it fits in well with our legal system, which adds a large number of *"you shall nots"* of its own—"You shall not drive at over 70 mph on the highway." And a Jewish teacher called Hillel, one of Jesus' contemporaries, expressed it all as clearly as anyone: "That which is hateful to you, do not do to your fellow man. That is the whole Law..."

> *The greatest Commandment is to love.*

When asked much the same question, though, Jesus gave a rather different response. The greatest commandment, he says, is to love: to love the Lord your God with all your heart and mind and soul and strength, and to love your neighbor as yourself.

In one sense it wasn't a very original answer: both commandments are to be found in the Old Testament (in Deuteronomy 6:5 and Leviticus

19:18 respectively), and the call to "love the Lord your God" was part of the so-called "Shema," a passage of Scripture that orthodox Jews still recite each morning and night. But it's probable that no one before Jesus had brought these verses together quite like this as a summary of what these commandments were about; and it's certain that no one before Jesus had so brilliantly modeled this more positive, proactive approach to godly living, truly practicing what he preached.

The *"you shalls"* of Jesus, of course, don't replace the *"you shall nots"* of the Ten Commandments. We love God by not cheating on God, by not taking God's name in vain, by honoring God's holy day; we love our neighbor by not stealing from her, not lying to her, not coveting what she has. But recognizing that love is at the heart of God's Commandments puts a quite different complexion on them, and on the way we're called to live. Not doing anyone any harm is just the start. Actively doing good is now the order of the day; and in Jesus' story of the Good Samaritan it's clear that doing good, loving our neighbor, applies not just to our nearest and dearest but to everyone whom God brings across our path (see Luke 10:25-37).

In short

It is easy to think we are being "good" if we do no harm. Jesus taught, and lived out, that what we do is more important than what we don't do. Jesus calls us actively to do good.

For discussion

- What gets in the way of us loving God and loving our neighbor? How might we try to change that; even in little ways?

- What does loving God really mean? And how do the words "heart," "mind," "soul," and "strength" fill out the picture?

- What kind of tribute/legacy would you like to leave behind?

How are we to love?

There is another difference, though, between Jesus' answer and that of Hillel, which is relevant today: because for Jesus, the first commandment was to love the Lord our God with all that we are and all that we have. Only then did he call us to love our neighbors as ourselves.

Loving God and loving neighbor belong together, and the best, most fruitful life is lived in loving communion with our Creator, as well as with our fellow human beings. "Lord, you have made us for yourself," as Augustine famously put it, "and our hearts are restless til they find their rest in you."

How then are we to love? That's a big theme in 1 John, one of the shorter letters towards the end of the New Testament. In chapters 3 and 4, John teaches us that love is about the way we act rather than what we say or how we feel; he emphasizes that love drives out fear; he goes on to remind us that love of God and love of neighbor belong together; and finally, two great statements: first, simply, "God is love" (4:16), and then, "We love because he first loved us" (4:19).

We receive, we give—that is the secret of a life that earns a different kind of tribute: not just "he never did anyone any harm," but rather "Well done, good and faithful servant: come and share your Master's happiness!" (Matthew 25:21).

> **In short**
> We cannot split our love of neighbor from our love of God. As 1 John says, "We love because he first loved us."

For discussion

- If love is more about how we act than how we feel, what might it mean to love our neighbor as ourselves?

- Does loving our neighbor always mean giving them what they ask for? How do we best respond to the poor or homeless in the street?

- What do you think John means when he writes that "perfect love drives out fear" (1 John 4:18)?

Concluding Prayer

Our Lord Jesus Christ said:

The first commandment is this:
"Hear, O Israel, the Lord our God is the only Lord.
You shall love the Lord your God with all your heart,
with all your soul, with all your mind,
and with all your strength."

The second is this: "Love your neighbor as yourself."
There is no other commandment greater than these.
On these two commandments hang all the law and the prophets.
Amen. Lord, have mercy.

Eternal God,
the light of the minds that know you,
the joy of the hearts that love you,
and the strength of the wills that serve you:
grant us so to know you
that we may truly love you,
so to love you that we may truly serve you,
whose service is perfect freedom;
through Jesus Christ our Lord.
Amen.

AFTER AUGUSTINE (354–430)

Sending Out

During this week reflect on what you have learned and explored in this session. How can your life reflect these two priorities of loving God and loving neighbor? What will that mean for the ways in which you spend your time?

These readings may help you in your reflection:

The reason for our loving God *is* God. God is the initiator of our love and its final goal. He is himself the occasion of human love; he gives us the power to love, and brings our desire to its consummation. God is loveable in himself, and gives himself to us as the object of our love. He desires that our love for him should bring us happiness, and not be arid and barren. His love for us opens up inside us the way to love, and is the reward of our own reaching out in love. How gently he leads us in love's way, how generously he returns the love we give, how sweet he is to those who wait for him!

BERNARD OF CLAIRVAUX (1090-1153)

In the evening of our lives, we shall be judged by love alone.

JOHN OF THE CROSS (1542-91)

To love at all is to be vulnerable. Love anything and your heart will certainly be wrung and possibly broken. If you want to make sure of keeping it intact, you must give your heart to no one, not even to an animal. Wrap it carefully around with hobbies and little luxuries; avoid all entanglements; lock it up safe in the casket or coffin of your selfishness. But in that casket—safe, dark, motionless, airless—it will change. It will not be broken; it will become unbreakable, impenetrable, and irredeemable.

C. S. LEWIS (1898-1963)

SESSION TWO:
REVERENCE

pilgrim

In this session we explore the vital importance of reverence and worship for God, and the danger of making idols of what we love.

Opening Prayers

Your word is a lantern to our feet
And a light upon our path.

PSALM 119:105

How shall a young man cleanse his way?
By keeping to your words.

With my whole heart I seek you;
let me not stray from your commandments.

I treasure your promise in my heart,
that I may not sin against you.

Blessed are you, O LORD;
instruct me in your statutes.

With my lips will I recite
all the judgments of your mouth.

I have taken greater delight in the way of your decrees
than in all manner of riches.

I will meditate on your commandments
and give attention to your ways.

My delight is in your statutes;
I will not forget your word.   PSALM 119:9-16

Almighty God,
We thank you for the gift of your holy word.
May it be a lantern to our feet,
a light to our path
and a strength to our lives.
Take us and use us
to love and serve all people
in the power of the Holy Spirit
and in the name of your Son,
Jesus Christ our Lord. **Amen.**

Describe, if you can, a time in your life when you have been moved to worship. It might be in a church service or in a different place.

Reflecting on Scripture

Reading

O sing to the LORD a new song; sing to the LORD, all the earth.
²Sing to the LORD, bless his name; tell of his salvation from day to day.
³Declare his glory among the nations, his marvelous works among all the peoples.
⁴For great is the LORD, and greatly to be praised; he is to be revered above all gods.
⁵For all the gods of the peoples are idols, but the LORD made the heavens.
⁶Honor and majesty are before him; strength and beauty are in his sanctuary.
⁷Ascribe to the LORD, O families of the peoples, ascribe to the LORD glory and strength.
⁸Ascribe to the LORD the glory due his name; bring an offering, and come into his courts.
⁹Worship the LORD in holy splendor; tremble before him, all the earth.
¹⁰Say among the nations, "The LORD is king! The world is firmly established; it shall never be moved. He will judge the peoples with equity."
¹¹Let the heavens be glad, and let the earth rejoice; let the sea roar, and all that fills it;
¹²let the field exult, and everything in it. Then shall all the trees of the forest sing for joy
¹³before the LORD; for he is coming, for he is coming to judge the earth. He will judge the world with righteousness, and the peoples with his truth.   PSALM 96

● Read the passage through once.

● Keep a few moments' silence.

● Read the passage a second time with different voices.

● Invite everyone to say aloud a word or phrase that strikes them.

● Read the passage a third time.

● Share together what this word or phrase might mean and what questions it raises.

Reflection   VICTORIA MATTHEWS

Icons and idols

Between 2010 and 2013, the Diocese of Christchurch, New Zealand, where I am Bishop, suffered more than 12,000 earthquakes and aftershocks causing death and destruction. Tens of thousands of homes were damaged or destroyed with the ground being compromised due to liquefaction and changes in the water table. The biggest challenge for the city and the nation, however, was the damage to the Christ Church Cathedral, the most visited church in the nation. Beginning on December 26, 2010, and worsening with every subsequent seismic event, the Cathedral was slowly but surely rocked to bits. When we announced that further deconstruction was deemed necessary for the sake of safety and for the retrieval of artifacts inside the ruin, lawsuits were brought to bear and public protests raged.

The question confronting the Christian community is when does a church building, consecrated to the glory of God, cease to be an icon and become an idol in the life of the community? An icon is a creation, an object that you gaze upon in order to glimpse God who is both ineffable and invisible. An idol is an object that is beautiful and often seductive in so far that an idol draws us away from the true worship of God.

Psalm 96:4 reminds us that it is the Lord who is worshipped. "For great is the Lord, and greatly to be praised; he is to be revered above all gods."

Christians are called to lead lives that worship God: Father, Son, and Holy Spirit, and to acknowledge God first. The Old Testament call for a tithe understands that it is the firstfruits of our lives that are for God, and not what is left over at the end of the harvest. Reverence is one way we pay homage to the Lord but whereas the tithe is a tenth, the New Testament clearly tells us that we owe all to God in Christ. We are called to acknowledge God first and not to replace our adoration of God with either activity or other objects of affection. If we wish to evaluate our life's stewardship, we would do well to examine how we spend our time and money.

In short

We are made to worship God and should do everything that we can to ensure that our worship is truly centered on God and that we are not distracted by anything else no matter how important it seems.

For discussion

- Do you think an icon can become an idol? What would need to happen for this to take place for a community or individual? What happens to worship when this happens?

- What are the most common idols in the society around us?

- Can reverence become crowded out of a life? What do we need to protect in order to preserve and enhance reverence in our life?

Practicing the presence of God

An additional insight from the earthquake experience here in New Zealand is that people quickly learned to worship in different spaces and places. The fortunate moved into their parish hall, but many found themselves in schools, funeral homes, and libraries. One year almost all Christmas services were held outside because the three earthquakes on December 23 did not allow enough time for buildings to be made safe for Christmas services. We now know we can worship anywhere and can rise to the occasion when thrown into unusual surroundings. People sit closer together by necessity and find they enjoy the enhanced sense of community. But what we do miss with the loss of dedicated sacred space is the possibility of slipping into church for prayer and quiet reflection. Gone are so many sacred spaces. Each space is used by many organizations. University lectures, community meetings, and 12-step organizations meet when and where they can. It raises the question, where does exclusive reverence for God happen? We can worship God anywhere, but does reverence for God suffer if a designated place for God is removed?

We live in the presence of God.

If we apply this idea of space and time to our calling to lead lives of reverence towards God, the challenge of giving time and a place to God arises. To lead lives of true reverence means living with a consciousness of the presence of God all the time. Just as top athletes never forget that their bodies are dedicated to sport, so the Christian is called to redeem time by living a life conscious of the presence and love of God through Christ in the power of the Spirit. This consciousness of God is nurtured by daily prayer and Scripture study and at least weekly attendance at Eucharistic worship.

Psalm 96 calls us to be aware that we live in the presence of God and God's handiwork. We observe the majesty of God and respond by voicing our adoration of the God who is in evidence all around us. "Ascribe to the Lord the glory due his name" (v. 8), and "tremble before him" (v. 9), reminds us that the majesty of the Lord is never to be taken for granted or overlooked. Every glimpse of the glory of God invites awe and wonder. Nor is it only the human population that praises God. "Let the field exult, and everything in it. Then shall all the trees of the forest sing for joy" (v. 12).

Reverence means living one's life in acknowledgement that God is sovereign and reigns over heaven and earth.

> **In short**
> God calls us to live constantly and consciously in God's presence and in awe of all that God has done—and continues to do—in the world.

For discussion

- Psalm 96 tells us about reverence being articulated and sung. What does silent reverence look and feel like?

- How might we practice the presence of God in each moment of our lives?

- Reverence also has to do with how we live our lives. If you examined your calendar and bank statements, what would you learn about what you revere?

Concluding Prayers

Lord, have mercy upon us,
and incline our hearts to keep your law.

You shall not make for yourself any idol,
whether in the form of anything that is in heaven above,
or that is on the earth beneath, or that is in the water under the earth.
You shall not bow down to them or worship them.
Lord, have mercy upon us,
and incline our hearts to keep your law.

O Lord our God,
grant us grace to desire you with our whole heart;
that so desiring, we may seek and find you;
and so finding, may love you;
and so loving, may hate those sins from which you have delivered us;
through Jesus Christ our Lord.
Amen.

Sending Out

During this week reflect on what you have learned and explored in this session. What pattern of worship and praise is right for you in the structure of your day and the pattern of your week?

These readings may help you in your reflection:

> Allow me to imitate the passion of my God. Earthly longings have been crucified in me; there is no spark of desire for mundane things, but only a murmur of living water that whispers within me, "Come to the Father."
>
> IGNATIUS OF ANTIOCH (*C.* 35–*C.* 107)

> The glory of God gives life; those who see God receive life. For this reason God, who cannot be grasped, comprehended or seen, allows himself to be seen, comprehended and grasped by men, that he may give life to those who see and receive him.
>
> IRENAEUS (*C.* 130–*C.* 200)

> God does not need golden cups, but he does need golden hearts.
>
> JOHN CHRYSOSTOM (*C.* 347–407)

> The heart is not pure if it worships God for a reward. What then? Shall we have no reward for the worship of God? Certainly we shall, but the reward will be God himself whom we worship. God's very self will be our reward.
>
> AUGUSTINE (354–430)

SESSION THREE:
REST

pilgrim

In this session we continue to explore the theme of reverence in the third commandment and the linked theme of rest and the Sabbath in the rhythm of our lives.

Opening Prayers

Your word is a lantern to my feet
And a light upon my path.

PSALM 119:105

Deal bountifully with your servant,
that I may live and keep your word.

Open my eyes, that I may see
the wonders of your law.

I am a stranger here on earth;
do not hide your commandments from me.

My soul is consumed at all times
with longing for your judgments.

You have rebuked the insolent;
cursed are they who stray from your commandments!

Turn from me shame and rebuke,
for I have kept your decrees.

Even though rulers sit and plot against me,
I will meditate on your statutes.

For your decrees are my delight;
and they are my counselors. PSALM 119:17-24

Almighty God,
We thank you for the gift of your holy word.
May it be a lantern to our feet,
a light to our path
and a strength to our lives.
Take us and use us
to love and serve all people
in the power of the Holy Spirit
and in the name of your Son,
Jesus Christ our Lord. **Amen.**

Conversation

When have you ever done or said something and used the authority of someone else to back you up? Have you ever tried to use God as your source of authority? Has that always been good or wise?

What is the longest number of days you have worked without taking a day off? How did you feel?

Reflecting on Scripture

Reading

Then God said, "Let us make humankind in our image, according to our likeness; and let them have dominion over the fish of the sea, and over the birds of the air, and over the cattle, and over all the wild animals of the earth, and over every creeping thing that creeps upon the earth." ^{27}So God created humankind in his image, in the image of God he created them; male and female he created them. ^{28}God blessed them, and God said to them, "Be fruitful and multiply, and fill the earth and subdue it; and have dominion over the fish of the sea and over the birds of the air and over every living thing that moves upon the earth." ^{29}God said, "See, I have given you every plant yielding seed that is upon the face of all the earth, and every tree with seed in its fruit; you shall have them for food. ^{30}And to every beast of the earth, and to every bird of the air, and to everything that creeps on the earth, everything that has the breath of life, I have given every green plant for food." And it was so. ^{31}God saw everything that he had made, and indeed, it was very good. And there was evening and there was morning, the sixth day.
2 ^{1}Thus the heavens and the earth were finished, and all their multitude. ^{2}And on the seventh day God finished the work that he had done, and he rested on the seventh day from all the work that he had done. ^{3}So God blessed the seventh day and hallowed

it, because on it God rested from all the work that he had done in creation. [4] These are the generations of the heavens and the earth when they were created.

GENESIS 1:26–2:4

Explanatory note

This passage helps us think about the basis for the third commandment, which we have summarized as "Do not dishonor the name of God." It also underlies the fourth commandment, "Remember the Sabbath and keep it holy."

Part of not dishonoring the name of God is remembering that we, both men and women, are made in the image of God (Genesis 1:26-27) and must treat ourselves and each other accordingly.

In reading this passage of Genesis, it is essential that we listen to what it says to us rather than impose our own questions on it. This passage is about very different matters than the "when?" and "how?" questions about the making of the universe that seem to preoccupy modern Western minds.

● Read the passage through once.

● Keep a few moments' silence.

● Read the passage a second time with different voices.

● Invite everyone to say aloud a word or phrase that strikes them.

● Read the passage a third time.

● Share together what this word or phrase might mean and what questions it raises.

Reflection
J. JOHN

An ordered universe

Because we hear so much talk about the universe being started by the "big bang" and shaped by "chaotic" and "random" processes it is very important that we take hold of the emphasis of the first pages of Genesis that the universe is ordered. This passage tells us that there is a vast and ordered hierarchy in the universe. Above absolutely everything and everyone is the majestic figure of God, the Creator and ruler of all things. God has created human beings with some responsibility over animals and plants. Genesis tells us that the universe is wonderfully and majestically constructed by God. Everything that exists is part of this extraordinary and breath-taking order.

If there is an order to both things and beings, this passage also teaches us that there is an ordering of *time*; we read here of the sixth and seventh days of creation. These are God's days, not ours, and as Augustine wrote 16 centuries ago, "What kind of days these are is difficult or even impossible for us to imagine" (*The City of God*, 11.6).

This passage gives the essential background to the third and fourth commandments. After the first two commandments, with their solemn rulings that we should worship God and reject all imitations, these next two seem almost commonplace. Indeed, if we consider them to involve nothing more than the rejection of blasphemous language and Sunday trading, then they are indeed trivial. The reality is, however, that both these commandments go deeper. The third commandment says that, precisely because God is Lord of the entire universe, we should not use his name lightly. Imagine how furious the President of the United States would be if, in some crooked marketing, someone put "By order of the President" on some pile of worthless junk. It is precisely this kind of abuse that this commandment rules against. We are to honor God in our worship and we are not to dishonor him in our lives. There are many things that we do and say to which we would be well advised not to add God's name. If there is mud in our lives, let us not drag God's name down into it! He is Lord of all and we should remember it with reverence.

> *We should not use God's name lightly.*

In short

We should associate God's name only with those things that are worthy of that name.

For discussion

- This passage in Genesis tells us that God is the maker of all things and that all that we have and are in life is God's gift. Is this a truth that we live out in our lives? If we really did live out this idea of God being Lord over everything that we are involved with, what would our attitude be to buying things, to how we manage the natural world, to how we treat the people who work for us?

- In anything we do there is good and bad. How do we give God the glory for the good without associating God with the bad parts?

Resting and looking forward in hope

The fourth commandment, which tells us to keep the Sabbath holy, refers back to God's supreme control over time. It is not just things that belong to God, it is time itself. God marked off six days of labor and then created a day in which he did not work. Precisely because God keeps the Sabbath, so should we. In the Old Testament the Sabbath is Saturday and focuses back to God's creation of the world. After the resurrection of Jesus the early Church developed a new perspective on the Sabbath, moving it to Sunday and shifting the focus forwards to the future remaking of a new heaven and earth with the coming of Christ. Paul and the writer to the Hebrews imply that the Old Testament Sabbath is a shadow of the eternal rest that believers in Jesus will enjoy (Colossians 2:16-17; Hebrews 4:8-10). If looking back with gratitude distinguishes the Old Testament perspective, looking forward with hope marks out the New Testament one. The wise Christian will hold both perspectives.

There are various interpretations of how practically we should keep a seventh day, but this commandment reminds us that we are to regularly set time aside and rest. Just as when traveling we set our clocks to local time, so as believers we should adopt God's time and pacing. In an age when many of us are frantically driven by agendas, to-do lists, and overloaded calendars, this gives us the helpful (and possibly life-saving) insight that God is the One who made and rules time. During our Sabbath rest we are to look back with thanksgiving to what God has done and look forward with hope to what God will do.

These two commandments form a pair; we are to remember that we should let God rule over our identity (who we are) and activity (what we do). God should be Lord of our ways and days.

In short

Part of living faithfully as Christians is setting time aside regularly to rest. This gives us time to give thanks for what God has done and to look forward to what he will do.

For discussion

- Do we consider each day as a gift from God? If we did believe this and carried out our beliefs, how would it change our lives?

- How can we make a sensible Sabbath? What impact would that have on family, friends, and ourselves?

Concluding Prayers

Lord, have mercy upon us,
and incline our hearts to keep your law.

Remember the Sabbath day, and keep it holy.
For six days you shall labor and do all your work.
But the seventh day is a Sabbath to the Lord your God.
Lord, have mercy upon us,
and incline our hearts to keep your law.

O Lord our God,
Give us by your Holy Spirit
A willing heart and a ready hand
to use all your gifts to your praise and glory. **Amen**.

THOMAS CRANMER (1489–1556)

Sending Out

Reflect this week on the way you have used (or possibly, abused) the authority that you have been given by God over things, people, and money. Have you honored God in what you did and said? How can you live in a way that will show more reverence to God?

Reflect this week on your use of time. Have you intentionally set aside time from your profession, pursuits, and pressures to be with God? Have you rested in God?

These readings may help you in your reflections:

> Eighty-six years I have served him, and he never did me any wrong. How can I blaspheme my King and my Savior?
>
> **POLYCARP AT HIS TRIAL (C. 160)**

> Keep close to Jesus.   **ABBA PAUL (4TH CENTURY)**

> If anyone would tell you the shortest, surest way to all happiness and perfection, he must tell you to make a rule to thank and praise God for everything that happens to you. Whatever seeming calamity happens to you, if you thank and praise God for it, it turns it into a blessing. Could you therefore work miracles, you could not do more for yourself than by this thankful spirit; it turns all that it touches into happiness.
>
> **WILLIAM LAW (1686–1761)**

> In the heavenly city there will be freedom of will. There that precept from the psalms will find fulfillment: "Be still and know that I am God." That will truly be the greatest of Sabbaths; a Sabbath that has no evening, the Sabbath that the Lord approved at the beginning of creation.
>
> **AUGUSTINE (354–430)**

> The point and the justification of leisure are not that the functionary should function faultlessly and without a breakdown, but that the functionary should continue to be a human being.
>
> **JOSEF PIEPER (1904–97)**

SESSION FOUR:
RESPECT

pilgrim

In this session we explore the theme of respect in the Christian life focused in the honor shown within the family and respecting the sanctity of life.

Opening Prayers

Your word is a lantern to our feet
And a light upon our path.

PSALM 119:105

My soul cleaves to the dust;
give me life according to your word.

I have confessed my ways, and you answered me;
instruct me in your statutes.

Make me understand the way of your commandments,
that I may meditate on your marvelous works.

My soul melts away for sorrow;
strengthen me according to your word.

Take from me the way of lying;
let me find grace through your law.

I have chosen the way of faithfulness;
I have set your judgments before me.

I hold fast to your decrees;
O LORD, let me not be put to shame.

I will run the way of your commandments,
for you have set my heart at liberty.   PSALM 119:25-32

Almighty God,
We thank you for the gift of your holy word.
May it be a lantern to our feet,
a light to our path
and a strength to our lives.
Take us and use us
to love and serve all people
in the power of the Holy Spirit
and in the name of your Son,
Jesus Christ our Lord. **Amen.**

Conversation

What kind of family did you grow up in? How was respect offered and received?

Reflecting on Scripture

Reading

Let love be genuine; hate what is evil, hold fast to what is good; [10]love one another with mutual affection; outdo one another in showing honor. [11]Do not lag in zeal, be ardent in spirit, serve the Lord. [12]Rejoice in hope, be patient in suffering, persevere in prayer. [13]Contribute to the needs of the saints; extend hospitality to strangers. [14] Bless those who persecute you; bless and do not curse them. [15]Rejoice with those who rejoice, weep with those who weep. [16]Live in harmony with one another; do not be haughty, but associate with the lowly; do not claim to be wiser than you are. [17]Do not repay anyone evil for evil, but take thought for what is noble in the sight of all. [18]If it is possible, so far as it depends on you, live peaceably with all. [19]Beloved, never avenge yourselves, but leave room for the wrath of God; for it is written, "Vengeance is mine, I will repay, says the Lord." [20]No, "if your enemies are hungry, feed them; if they are thirsty, give them something to drink; for by doing this you will heap burning coals on their heads." [21]Do not be overcome by evil, but overcome evil with good.

ROMANS 12:9-21

Explanatory note

Saints—this word now has a very specific meaning, often used to describe those who have been recognized by the Roman Catholic Church as being holy, but Paul used the word for all Christians, and it is what he means here.

The word "noble" doesn't quite capture the word used here. It can be translated as fine, beautiful, magnificent, lovely, and good as well as noble.

The quotation about vengeance comes from Deuteronomy 32:35 and Paul uses it to remind us that judgment belongs to God; we are to act very differently.

- Read the passage through once.
- Keep a few moments' silence.
- Read the passage a second time with different voices.
- Invite everyone to say aloud a word or phrase that strikes them.
- Read the passage a third time.
- Share together what this word or phrase might mean and what questions it raises.

Reflection ALAN SMITH

Honoring our parents

Most of us like to be respected. When our opinions are taken seriously we feel that we matter and are making a contribution. If we are ignored, we easily feel demeaned and excluded. However, in the Bible the fifth and sixth of the Ten Commandments are not primarily about our right to receive respect. Instead they ask us *to give respect to others*.

First, we are commanded to respect our parents: "*honor your father and mother.*" In ancient society three or even four generations might live in the same household. Meals were eaten together and work shared, with each member of the family having a different but important role. Children of whatever age looked to their parents' guidance to make this web of relationships and responsibilities work.

The call to respect is not just for practical reasons. We were each brought into being through the bodily union of our parents. Our parents were reflecting and sharing in the creative work of God. Throughout our childhood, our parents (or other adults who loved and raised us) represented God in the way they cared, nurtured, and taught us. In the Old Testament, therefore, to respect your parents was to respect God. Conversely, to dishonor your parents was to dishonor God. Significantly, the fifth commandment is the only one to include a promise "...that you may live long in the land the Lord your God is giving you."

It is important to note that the commandment is not to love our father and mother, but to *honor* them. Sometimes we cannot love one or both parents, and when this occurs it can induce terrible feelings of guilt. God does not demand the impossible, but God does require that we honor those who gave us life. We need to release our parents from unrealistic expectations and respect them for who they are—fallible men and women who make mistakes like us.

> **In short**
> Respecting your parents and respecting God are linked in the Old Testament. We are not required to love our father and mother, but to honor them.

For discussion

- Who do you respect and why? What causes you to lose respect for someone?
- What does "honor your father and mother" mean today when most family members do not live together in the same home and may live in another part of the country?

Respecting life

Second, we are commanded to respect the lives of others and, in particular, not to commit murder. God is the source and giver of life, and we are to respect it. The commandment enshrines a fundamental principle for the health of any society. The alternative is fear and anarchy, especially for the weak and the vulnerable who cannot defend themselves. The Hebrew word here is not "kill" but "murder," and as such has a specific meaning. In the Old Testament the term applied to someone who took revenge on their enemy. Even in earliest times it was recognized that someone might kill another person accidentally, and in such cases they were given a place of sanctuary. Nor did the commandment apply to those who were protecting themselves (Exodus 22:2), or to capital punishment (Exodus 21:12), or exclude the terrible realities of war (Deuteronomy 20).

Several centuries later Jesus expanded the meaning and scope of the sixth commandment in these terms:

> "You have heard that it was said to those of ancient times, 'You shall not murder'; and 'whoever murders shall be liable to judgment.' But I say to you that if you are angry with a brother or sister, you will be liable to judgment; and if you insult a brother or sister, you will be liable to the council; and if you say, 'You fool,' you will be liable to the hell of fire."
>
> MATTHEW 5:21-22

Jesus knew only too well that anger, if left to fester, could turn into violence and lead to murderous acts. For this reason he forbade his followers from using derogatory names for one another and challenged them to examine their thoughts and motives. Destructive feelings need to be expelled before they take root in our lives and poison relationships.

Destructive feelings need to be expelled.

When we turn to chapter 12 of Paul's Letter to the Romans, we find no less than 21 commands, each of which is an invitation to respect God and our neighbor. They are ways in which the grace of God can transform our lives. We cannot demand that others respect us, but by freely giving respect to other people, we demonstrate that we ourselves are people worthy of respect.

In short

Jesus reminds us in the Gospels that the commandment that we should not murder is about much more than simply not killing people; it involves keeping our anger in check and treating one another with deep respect.

For discussion

- Jesus says that we should not even have angry thoughts about another person. How can we channel our negative feelings in a more positive way, particularly when we don't respect someone?

- How can we put the 21 commands in Romans 12:9-21 into action?

Concluding Prayer

Honor your father and your mother.
Lord, have mercy upon us,
and incline our hearts to keep your law.

You shall not murder.
Lord, have mercy upon us,
and incline our hearts to keep your law.

Sending Out

During this week reflect on what you have learned and explored in this session. Reflect on the way in which being a disciple might lead to change within your family and change in your conversation.

These readings may help you in your reflection:

Jesus says, "Anyone who hates his brother or sister is a murderer." Someone who hates another may not be shut up in prison, but they are imprisoned by guilt. Their heart has become a prison. God has given you time and opportunity to amend. God spares you; so spare others. Wake up and seek reconciliation with them.

CAESARIUS OF ARLES (*C.* 470–*C.* 543)

Children love their parents, but sometimes their eyes stray to the inheritance they hope to receive and end up respecting them more than they actually love them because they are frightened of being disinherited. Love which is motivated by the hope of getting something is suspect. It is flawed and will collapse if the object of its hope is withdrawn. It is sullied because it is seeking for something other than itself. Pure love is never mercenary.

BERNARD OF CLAIRVAUX (1090–1153)

God's plans are better than our own, and he has ordained that the training-place for his human creatures should be the home; the training-place for parents as well as children. Our task is to restore true family life for it is God's own institution, and therefore a divine thing. There are two divine institutions in the world: the Church and the home. The home is God's institution as truly as is the Church: let that be the truth that we proclaim!

MARY SUMNER (1828–1921)

The primary principle of Christian ethics and Christian politics must be respect for every person simply as a person. If each man and woman is a child of God, whom God loves and for whom Christ died, then there is in each a worth absolutely independent of all usefulness to society. The person is primary, not the society; the State exists for the citizen, not the citizen for the State.

WILLIAM TEMPLE (1881–1944)

RIGHTEOUSNESS

pilgrim

In this session we explore the commandments about adultery and theft and their implications for our daily lives.

Opening Prayers

Your word is a lantern to our feet
And a light upon our path.

PSALM 119:105

Teach me, O Lord, the way of your statutes,
and I shall keep it to the end.

Give me an understanding, and I shall keep your law;
I shall keep it with all my heart.

Make me go in the path of your commandments,
for that is my desire.

Incline my heart to your decrees
and not to unjust gain.

Turn my eyes from watching what is worthless;
give me life in your ways.

Fulfill your promise to your servant,
which you make to those who fear you.

Turn away the reproach which I dread,
because your judgments are good.

Behold, I long for your commandments;
in your righteousness preserve my life.   PSALM 119:33-40

Almighty God,
We thank you for the gift of your holy word.
May it be a lantern to our feet,
a light to our path
and a strength to our lives.
Take us and use us
to love and serve all people
in the power of the Holy Spirit
and in the name of your Son,
Jesus Christ our Lord. **Amen.**

Conversation

How easy do you find it to be good? Where are the points of struggle in these years of your life?

Reflecting on Scripture

Reading

"You have heard that it was said, 'You shall not commit adultery.' 28But I say to you that everyone who looks at a woman with lust has already committed adultery with her in his heart. 29If your right eye causes you to sin, tear it out and throw it away; it is better for you to lose one of your members than for your whole body to be thrown into hell. 30And if your right hand causes you to sin, cut it off and throw it away; it is better for you to lose one of your members than for your whole body to go into hell. 31It was also said, 'Whoever divorces his wife, let him give her a certificate of divorce.' 32But I say to you that anyone who divorces his wife, except on the ground of unchastity, causes her to commit adultery; and whoever marries a divorced woman commits adultery. 33Again, you have heard that it was said to those of ancient times, 'You shall not swear falsely, but carry out the vows you have made to the Lord.'"

MATTHEW 5:27-33

Explanatory note

The question of when and why you could get divorced was commonly discussed at the time of Jesus. Jesus' view on the matter was neither the most harsh nor the most lenient.

● Read the passage through once.

● Keep a few moments' silence.

● Read the passage a second time with different voices.

- Invite everyone to say aloud a word or phrase that strikes them.
- Read the passage a third time.
- Share together what this word or phrase might mean and what questions it raises.

Reflection   LUCY WINKETT

Adultery and stealing: two forms of greed

In the church where I'm rector, two boards depict the Ten Commandments. I saw a man stop to read them. He saw me approaching and rather ruefully said, "Well, I've broken all of those." Then, after a pause, he looked again, "Oh, except murder."

Thinking about righteousness and what that might look like in our lives can make us feel anxious. It reminds us of being told off. Hearts beat a little faster as we read, "You shall not steal." We wonder if it really means the stapler we borrowed from work and haven't got around to returning. But righteousness is not so much about being told off as an invitation to live life abundantly and well. The Ten Commandments are about individual flourishing and building strong community, reminding us of our interdependence. These two commandments in particular address us as people with responsibilities to others, who know what it means to belong. Adultery is committed when a person who has pledged himself or herself to someone else breaks that pledge. Stealing betrays a disregard for the idea that property can belong to someone else.

It's a narrow view of adultery to define it only as sex between a married person and someone they are not married to. Jesus doesn't define it like this. One of his much used sayings is here in Matthew: "You have heard that it was said... But I say to you..." He takes what he says are narrow interpretations and transforms them by emphasizing that the spirit of the law is more important than the letter. Jesus dramatically widens and deepens the definition of adultery by saying that seeing someone as an object of lust rather than as a whole human being is adulterous in itself. Carol Ann Duffy expresses the disorientating and potentially cataclysmic effects of this in her poem, "Adultery": *paranoia for lunch, too much to drink, as a hand on your thigh tilts the restaurant.*

In conversation with couples preparing for marriage, I often ask them what strategies they have in place now for when they fall for someone else. Young people now can expect to live to 100 and so in a long life it's almost bound to happen. Whether the danger moments involve alcohol, being away from home, feeling ignored by a partner, busyness at work, children, or feeling bored with a job, being able to be honest with ourselves means that our prayers have a good chance of being real. The Commandments force us to face ourselves as we really are.

In short

Adultery and stealing are about breaking our responsibilities to others, not simply to ourselves. Being honest about possibilities gives us strength to resist them.

For discussion

● What does the word "righteousness" mean to you? Does it include your responsibilities to others?

● One writer says that one of the principal causes of the breakdown of so many marriages is "a lack of the spirit of obedience," which emerges from deep listening to the other. Do you agree? What are the barriers to listening?

Loved too much to be left as we are

Stealing, like adultery, can be described as a form of greed. Is stealing ever justified? Desperation can provide a powerful motive. Is it a different form of lust: for sensation, or excitement; even for the fear of being found out? When we regularly indulge this impulse, it easily becomes a habit of our heart. We can quite easily get to the point that it stops being on our radar of what is right or wrong. Different people will draw different lines. In regarding some things as "perks" from hotels or work, by using the language of "borrowing" rather than stealing, we set aside the astonishing truth that everything we have, everyone we have loved, the unique mix of our own life experience and all our possessions, all of it is a gift from God.

They are a firm and friendly arm around the shoulder.

How we feel about commandments often depends on our personality and experience. Some of us are generally rule keepers and some of us are rule breakers. Reflecting on our whole life experience is vital in developing our own relationship with God, not least because it's in our mistakes that we lose a measure of control. In dealing with those mistakes, even when they're made willfully, God can communicate more powerfully than when we're all sorted out.

Although they might feel like it sometimes, I don't think these commandments are impersonal instructions shouted at us from far away. They are a firm and friendly arm around the shoulder. "This is how to live. Do this." They're signposts, indicating a path towards a deep, loving and generous realization of the struggles that are part of the human condition. As the profound French expression has it, "to know all is to forgive all." These commandments, to which we have to return time and time again, every day, every hour sometimes, assure us that there is integrity in attempting the journey at all. And they encourage us to know that we are loved and accepted by God in Christ exactly as we are, but are loved too much to be left that way.

> **In short**
> These commandments are signposts, encouraging us to be honest with others and ourselves, true to our commitments and confident in God's grace and love.

For discussion

- What is the most common form of stealing in your experience?

- Do you think you are naturally a rule breaker or a rule keeper? How does that affect your view of these commandments?

- How do you respond to the idea that God loves us too much to leave us as we are?

Concluding Prayer

You shall not commit adultery.
Lord, have mercy upon us,
and incline our hearts to keep your law.

You shall not steal.
Lord, have mercy upon us,
and incline our hearts to keep your law.

Sending Out

During this week reflect on what you have learned and explored in this session and its lessons for your life in the near and distant future.

These readings may help you in your reflection:

> Christians marry like everyone else. They beget children, but they do not abandon them at birth. They will share their table with you, but not their marriage bed. They are in the world, but they refuse to conform to the ways of the world.
>
> *LETTER TO DIOGNETUS* (C. 150)

In matters of judgment, second thoughts are invariably right; in matters of conscience, never.

JOHN HENRY NEWMAN (1801–90)

One of the principal causes of the breakdown of so many marriages is a lack of the spirit of obedience. No word in the religious vocabulary is so much misunderstood by our contemporaries. Obedience is in essence the capacity to listen to the other. We stray from God when we lose this attentiveness and no amount of talking or thinking about God can truly substitute for this openness to him. The Latin root of obedience is *ob-audire*, to hear, to listen. We are to be listeners. Obedience then is deep sensitivity to the other: the readiness to think, in the first place, of the other and not of oneself. It is impossible for us to love one another unless we serve one another.

JOHN MAIN (1926–82)

We must ask about our relationship to our bodies, about Paul's fear of the body, and the hatred of the body which since Augustine and his doctrine of the drives has tormented Christianity. It turned into fatal mistrust of the body and we must replace it with a new way of dealing with our own bodies, which I would want to term friendship. And just as trust comes first in any friendship, so too trust in our bodies will be the important step we need to take towards such a friendly relationship which is not determined by exploitation, indifference, or anxiety.

ELISABETH MOLTMANN-WENDEL (1926–)

Most of us in the Western world are more physically mobile than ever; we expect change and variety in our work; we have less and less interest or commitment as a society in the ideal of sexual faithfulness; we are entertained by deliberately hectic and rapid images. It isn't difficult in this world to start imagining that the body is really a sort of tool for the will to use in getting its entertainment and satisfaction, its sense of power and fulfillment … Christianity encourages me to be faithful to the body that I am …

ROWAN WILLIAMS (1950–)

SESSION SIX:
RELIABILITY

pilgrim

In this final session we explore the damage and the dangers of dishonesty and covetousness.

Opening Prayers

Your word is a lantern to my feet
And a light upon my path.

PSALM 119:105

Let your loving-kindness come to me, O LORD,
and your salvation, according to your promise.

Then shall I have a word for those who taunt me,
because I trust in your words.

Do not take the word of truth out of my mouth,
for my hope is in your judgments.

I shall continue to keep your law;
I shall keep it for ever and ever.

I will walk at liberty,
because I study your commandments.

I will tell of your decrees before kings
and will not be ashamed.

I delight in your commandments,
which I have always loved.

I will lift up my hands to your commandments,
and I will meditate on your statutes.

PSALM 119:41-48

Almighty God,
We thank you for the gift of your holy word.
May it be a lantern to our feet,
a light to our path
and a strength to our lives.
Take us and use us
to love and serve all people
in the power of the Holy Spirit

and in the name of your Son,
Jesus Christ our Lord. **Amen.**

Conversation

Recalling today's news headlines, which possessions, positions, and relationships would you say are most prized by society? What do you most covet in your life? What do you most value in your life?

Reflecting on Scripture

Reading

Later the following events took place: Naboth the Jezreelite had a vineyard in Jezreel, beside the palace of King Ahab of Samaria. ²And Ahab said to Naboth, "Give me your vineyard, so that I may have it for a vegetable garden, because it is near my house; I will give you a better vineyard for it; or, if it seems good to you, I will give you its value in money." ³But Naboth said to Ahab, "The LORD forbid that I should give you my ancestral inheritance." ⁴Ahab went home resentful and sullen because of what Naboth the Jezreelite had said to him; for he had said, "I will not give you my ancestral inheritance." He lay down on his bed, turned away his face, and would not eat. ⁵His wife Jezebel came to him and said, "Why are you so depressed that you will not eat?" ⁶He said to her, "Because I spoke to Naboth the Jezreelite and said to him, 'Give me your vineyard for money; or else, if you prefer, I will give you another vineyard for it'; but he answered, 'I will not give you my vineyard.'" ⁷His wife Jezebel said to him, "Do you now govern Israel? Get up, eat some food, and be cheerful; I will give you the vineyard of Naboth the Jezreelite." ⁸So she wrote letters in Ahab's name and sealed them with his seal; she sent the letters to the elders and the nobles who lived with Naboth in his city. ⁹She wrote in the letters, "Proclaim a fast, and seat Naboth at the head

of the assembly; [10]seat two scoundrels opposite him, and have
them bring a charge against him, saying, 'You have cursed God
and the king.' Then take him out, and stone him to death." [11]The
men of his city, the elders and the nobles who lived in his city, did
as Jezebel had sent word to them. Just as it was written in the
letters that she had sent to them, [12]they proclaimed a fast and
seated Naboth at the head of the assembly. [13]The two scoundrels
came in and sat opposite him; and the scoundrels brought a
charge against Naboth, in the presence of the people, saying,
"Naboth cursed God and the king." So they took him outside the
city, and stoned him to death. [14]Then they sent to Jezebel, saying,
"Naboth has been stoned; he is dead." [15]As soon as Jezebel heard
that Naboth had been stoned and was dead, Jezebel said to Ahab,
"Go, take possession of the vineyard of Naboth the Jezreelite,
which he refused to give you for money; for Naboth is not alive,
but dead.'" [16]As soon as Ahab heard that Naboth was dead, Ahab
set out to go down to the vineyard of Naboth the Jezreelite, to
take possession of it.

1 KINGS 21:1-16

Explanatory note

When the people of God arrived in the promised land, the land was shared equally
between tribes and within tribes between extended families. As a result, people
believed the land had been given to them by God. This explains Naboth's attitude here.

● Read the passage through once.

● Keep a few moments' silence.

● Read the passage a second time with different voices.

● Invite everyone to say aloud a word or phrase that strikes them.

● Read the passage a third time.

● Share together what this word or phrase might mean and what
  questions it raises.

Jealousy and its consequences

Ahab desires a significant vineyard from its owner Naboth, who declines the offer of a swap. Ahab begins an almighty sulk, and his wife Jezebel, a shrewd political operator, tells a lie, and stirs up local ill feeling towards Naboth. Naboth is stoned to death, and the vineyard taken by Ahab.

Coveting another's possessions and bearing false witness, the subjects of the last two of the Ten Commandments, are at the heart of this ancient tale, and of many a modern story of gang warfare or political intrigue. As with any despotic ruler, media mogul, or drug baron, Ahab's longing to dominate a piece of turf, linked through heritage and kinship to power in the community, goes beyond merely wanting possessions. Instead, it becomes an all-consuming acquisitiveness, which quickly eats away at his sense of status and worth, and leads to a petulant withdrawal from social interaction. And, as with any political fixer, spin doctor, or gangster's moll, Jezebel's modus operandi is to plant a lie and then to stand back silently, while others compound her actions. Naboth pays the price of the lie with his life.

Whereas the focus of the second to eighth commandments is more about our actions, these last two are more about the kind of change of heart that will need to come about if we are to follow the first commandment, to love the Lord our God with our whole selves: inwardly and outwardly. Picking up this emphasis, Jesus reinterpreted the Commandments in Matthew 5, highlighting inner attitudes and virtues, rather than strict outer observance, as the foundations of godly living on which his disciples would want to build their lives.

Between them, these commandments not to covet and not to bear false witness are at the heart of this inner way of being which we will long to adopt as a loving response to divine grace. To covet is to be unable to see the value of what God has already given us, and to allow envy or disappointment at our perceived relative lack of status to devalue our own worth in the abundantly generous economy of God's love. Covetousness goes beyond acquiring an object of beauty, worth, or usefulness; beyond seeking a relationship that brings pleasure; beyond working to improve one's life chances. It becomes instead an insatiable craving which wipes out the value of what we already have. Although tabloids and lifestyle magazines earn their circulation figures by serving up a regular diet of envy-inducing stories and photographs, the cost to their readers is a diminution of their own lives. As the seventeenth-century Episcopal writer George Herbert expressed it, "All covet, all lose."

> **In short**
> These final two commandments are about our inner attitudes, a change of heart, to be truthful and to be content.

For discussion

- A playful lie is one that is believable but intended for amusement. An officious lie, sometimes called a white lie, does no harm. An injurious lie is intended to hurt someone. Think of an example of each. Is any form of lying OK?

- If a senior manager at work sought to place the blame for the organization's failings on another colleague, when you knew that the manager himself was in a large part to blame, would you speak up? What might be the costs?

Bearing false witness sets us apart from the truth and justice that govern God's loving engagement with the world. Thomas Aquinas defined lying as "a statement at variance with the mind," but active lying is not the only form of false witness: gossiping, allowing misinformation to circulate through and around us, or giving false testimony in court, are actions that similarly break the bonds of community. NBC News anchor Brian Williams' purported false memories of being shot down in a helicopter with his news crew more than a decade ago in Iraq made the headlines in 2015. Williams, to the shock of many, did not respond to the revelation that his story was untrue with contrition and admission of the lie, nor did he seek true forgiveness for what was, to many, a failed attempt at self-aggrandizement. Soon after, he was removed from his position. Truth telling is at the heart of the relationships of trust that we have with each other and, ultimately, with God.

Benedict, writing about the values of community life, placed a high value within his monastery on stability, to which all monks were asked to "bind" themselves. Reliability, integrity, and consistency were the markers of such stability, and necessary, even if not sufficient, qualities for a life ordered around the service of God. Although Christians do not earn salvation, since only the love of God expressed through Jesus Christ brings us back into perfect unity with our Creator, all Christians will want to work to develop a stable core of values and principles that attest to their faith. Ahab's covetousness and Jezebel's lies are the antithesis of this kind of principled, ordered, and faithful community life, in which all are enabled to flourish. Showing consistency between our inner thoughts and outer actions, and therefore between what we believe and who we are, is the life-giving discipline that holds us fast when we choose to travel with God.

In short
Seeking to be truthful and to be content are part of a stable core of values that all Christians need to embrace.

For discussion

- Think of one thing in your life that you could change from a grumble to a moment of gratitude.

- What patterns of life would best support you in being a reliable and consistent person, showing integrity across your inner thoughts and outer actions? What will you need to change to move towards this pattern of life?

- Which of the Ten Commandments have you thought most deeply about in this short series?

Concluding Prayer

You shall not bear false witness.
Lord, have mercy upon us,
and incline our hearts to keep your law.

You shall not covet.
Lord, have mercy upon us,
and write all these your laws in our hearts.

Sending Out

During this week reflect on what you have learned and explored in this session. Look back over the commandments we have studied. Try to find some space and quiet and reflect on how you want your life to change and be changed. Seek God's grace in prayer for these changes. Reflect on whether there are any practical steps to be taken.

These readings may help you in your reflection:

> It is incumbent on every lover of truth, at whatever personal cost, even if their life is at stake, to choose to do and to speak only what is right.
>
> JUSTIN (*C*. 100–*C*. 165)

> Let us never misuse what has been given to us by the gift of God. If we do, we shall hear Peter say: "Be ashamed of yourselves for holding on to what belongs to somebody else. Resolve to imitate God's justice and no one will be poor." Let us never labor to heap up and hoard riches while others remain in need.
>
> GREGORY OF NAZIANZUS (329–89)

> Would you know what sort of clothing the Lord prefers you to wear? Prudence, justice, moderation, courage. These four virtues should fill your horizon. Think of them as a four-horse team bearing you, Christ's charioteer, along at full speed to your goal. No

necklace can be more precious than these; no gems could create a brighter galaxy. So let them be the jewelry you wear and the garments with which you clothe yourself, for they will protect you on every side. They are your defense and your glory; for each of these gems God turns into a shield.

JEROME (342–420)

Envy comes from people's ignorance of, or lack of belief in, their own gifts.

JEAN VANIER (1928–)

The very fact that the lust that grips so many lives is never satiated suggests that lust has become a form of greed. For if any one characteristic is to be associated with greed it is the presumption that no matter how much we may have we need "more." We need more because we cannot be sure that what we have is secure. So the more we have the more we must have in order to secure what we have.

STANLEY HAUERWAS (1940–)

NOTES

The Commandments quoted on pages 13–14 and in the opening worship are taken from the translations used in the Book of Common Prayer.

Session One
Augustine (354–430) (adapted from).
Bernard of Clairvaux (1090–1153), *On the Love of God*, 7.
John of the Cross (1542–91), *Spiritual Sentences and Maxims*.
C. S. Lewis (1898–1963), *The Four Loves*, Oxford, Geoffrey Bles, 1958.

Session Two
St Augustine (354–430), *Exposition of Psalm 55*, 17.
John Chrysostom (347–407), *Homilies on St Matthew's Gospel*, 50, 4.
Ignatius of Antioch (c. 35–c. 107), *Letter to the Romans*, 7.
Irenaeus (c. 130– c. 200).

Session Three
Abba Paul (4th century), *Sayings of the Desert Fathers and Mothers*, Paul the Great, 4.
St Augustine (354–430), *The City of God*, XXII, 30.
Thomas Cranmer (1489–1556),
William Law (1686–1761), *A Serious Call to a Devout and Holy Life*.
Josef Pieper (1904–97), *Leisure: the Basis of Culture*, Munich, 1948; ET, London, Faber and Faber, 1952.
Polycarp at his trial (c. 160), *The Martyrdom of Polycarp*, 9.

Session Four
Bernard of Clairvaux (1090–1153), *On the Song of Songs*, 33, ii.
Caesarius of Arles (c. 470–c. 543), *Sermon on Fraternal Harmony*, 1.
Mary Sumner (1828–1921), Founder of the Mothers' Union.
William Temple (1881–1944), *Christianity and Social Order*, London, Penguin, 1942.

Session Five
Carol Ann Duffy, "Adultery," *Love Poems*, London, Picador, 2010.
Letter to Diognetus (c. 150), 5.
John Main (1926–82), *The Joy of Being*, selected by Clare Hallward, London, Darton, Longman and Todd, 1989, p. 14.
Elisabeth Moltmann-Wendel (1926–), *Rediscovering Friendship*, London, SCM Press, 2000.
John Henry Newman (1801–90).
Rowan Williams (1950–), *Silence and Honey Cakes: The Wisdom of the Desert*, Oxford, Lion Hudson, 2003, pp. 91–3.

Session Six
Gregory of Nazianzus (329–89), Oration "On the love of the poor."
Stanley Hauerwas (1940–), "Never enough: Why greed is still so deadly," ABC Religion and Ethics, October 3, 2011.
Jerome (342–420), *Letter* 52, 13.
Justin (c. 100–c. 165), *First Apology*, 2, 6, 11.
Jean Vanier (1928–), "One Heart, One Soul, One Spiri," in *Community and Growth*, New Jersey, Paulist Press, 1989, p. 51.